# Stories of
# GHOSTS

### Russell Punter

## Illustrated by
## Mike Phillips

Reading Consultant: Alison Kelly
University of Surrey Roehampton

# Contents

# Chapter 1

# The story of Shiverham Hall

Have a frightful stay, madam.

Shiverham Hall was a hotel with a difference. All the guests were dead.

Ghosts came from the spirit world to be greeted by Shiverham's spooky staff.

There were twenty-two ice-cold bedrooms...

Aahh, I..I..lovely.

a poltergeist-powered jacuzzi...

and a string quartet playing haunting tunes.

4

No living soul dared visit the hotel. It was far too creepy. The ghosts were left in peace.

Then, one afternoon, the hotel's deathly hush was shattered.

SLAM!

Most of the ghosts were napping. Mr. Quiver, the hotel manager, had come down for a glass of water.

Suddenly, a round-faced man flung open the front door and strode up to the reception desk.

"This is just what I've been looking for," he boomed.

A tall, thin man scuttled in after him.

"Um, are you sure, Mr. Slate?" he asked nervously.

"Of course I'm sure, Simkins," barked Slate. "This will make the perfect site for my new hotel. I've had it all designed."

Slate proudly spread out a large plan in front of his assistant. Behind them, Mr. Quiver sneaked up to get a better look.

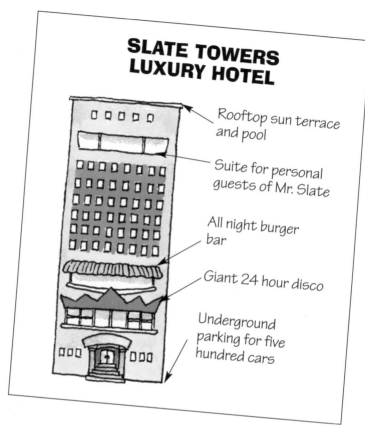

## SLATE TOWERS LUXURY HOTEL

Rooftop sun terrace and pool

Suite for personal guests of Mr. Slate

All night burger bar

Giant 24 hour disco

Underground parking for five hundred cars

Mr. Quiver was horrified. "I'll have this place demolished in no time," Slate went on. "But perhaps I'll look around and see if there's anything worth saving first."

"Don't be too long," gulped Simkins. "They say the place is haunted."

"Ridiculous!" cried Slate. "Ghosts don't exist. And I'll stay the night to prove it."

"We don't exist, eh?" thought Mr. Quiver, as he floated upstairs.

Minutes later, he gathered the hotel staff together. No one was happy about Slate's plans.

"We'll never get any peace in his noisy new hotel," wailed Charlie the waiter.

"And where will our ghostly guests go?" asked Elsie the maid.

"Slate will have to be frightened off," said Mr. Quiver. "As soon as it gets dark, we'll start haunting."

Slate was climbing the rickety stairs to bed, when Mr. Quiver appeared in front of him.

Slate looked a little surprised. But then he shrugged.

"Out of my way, potato head!" he shouted.

11

Mr. Quiver had never been so insulted in his life. Or his death.

But the ghosts weren't finished yet. As Slate brushed his teeth, Igor the porter popped up through the plughole.

The staff didn't give up.
That night, Slate was visited
by a stream of ghosts...

Elsie brought the
bed sheets to life.

Charlie rattled
a ghostly tea
tray next to
Slate's pillow.

Cora the cook
sent possessed
pots flying
through the air.

13

Even the hotel guests tried to put the shivers up the unwelcome visitor.

Sir Gauntlet showed off his battle scars.

Lord Doublet lost his head.

And Miss Gauntly, the wailing lady, moaned the entire night.

But none of them could raise a single goosebump.

Next morning, Mr. Quiver listened in on Slate's meeting with Simkins.

"You were right," said Slate. "This place *is* full of ghosts."

"R..r..really?" stuttered Simkins, nervously. "So you'll forget your plans?"

"No way!" said Slate. "People will pay even more to stay in a luxury *haunted* hotel. I'll soon have those spooks hard at work."

I'll make a fortune!

Within minutes, the ghosts' tragic tale appeared on the Spirit World Wide Web.

# Ghosts' Online Gazette

## SO LONG SHIVERHAM!

**HISTORIC HOTEL TO BE FLATTENED - STAFF FACE SLAVERY TO SLATE**

The staff of Shiverham Hall are to become a 'tourist attraction' in a new hotel built by Percival Slate.

*Percival Slate*

It looked as if the ghosts' peaceful life was coming to an end. Next day, the staff watched from the shadows as Slate dreamed of what was to come.

Suddenly, a spooky figure appeared from nowhere.

"Yoo hoo!" she cried.

"Aha!" said Slate. "Another spook, and a very ugly one."

"Don't you recognize me Percy?" said the ghost. "It's me, your Great Aunt Mabel!"

Slate's ghostly aunt planted a slobbery wet kiss on his cheek. Slate's face turned bright red.

"I read all about you on The Ghosts' Gazette website," said Mabel. "So I've decided to come and live in your lovely new hotel."

Live here? B..b..but...

"I'll look after you, Percy," cried Mabel. "I'll feed you up on my special cabbage soup and I'll make sure you get a bath and a big kiss every bedtime!"

Slate had been terrified of his aunt when she was alive. Now she was even scarier.

"I've ch..changed my mind," he stammered, tore up his plans, and ran.

All the ghosts cheered. Mr. Quiver approached Great Aunt Mabel and bowed.

"Thank you, madam," he said. "Please stay as our guest for as long as you want – for free."

## Chapter 2

# School for spooks

Tammy Tremble was learning how to be a ghost. But her first week at Creepy College had been a disaster.

Things began badly on
Monday. Miss Hover, the
poltergeist, had shown the
class how to make objects
float in mid-air...

Keep them nice
and high.

I'm totally
unmoved.

...but Tammy couldn't seem to
get anything off the ground.

22

On Tuesday, Tammy took a fright class with Miss Screech. But no one was remotely scared by her efforts – not even Marley, the school cat.

On Wednesday came Miss
Faintly's lesson on how to
walk through walls. The rest
of the class slid through with
ease and received gold stars.

The only stars Tammy
saw were the ones
spinning around her
swollen head.

24

By the end of the week, Tammy was the unhappiest pupil in the school.

I'm never going to make the ghostly grade.

While the rest of the college went on a haunting field trip, Tammy had to stay behind and study her spookery.

Slowly, Tammy's skills improved – but could she keep them up?

She was taking a well-earned rest, when a cloud of smoke wafted by.

Marley the cat had knocked over one of Miss Screech's torches. The school was on fire! Tammy had to call for help.

The only phone in the school was in Miss Creepy's study. When Tammy got there, she found the door locked.

There was only one thing to do. Thinking back to Miss Faintly's lesson, Tammy crossed her fingers and charged at the door.

To her amazement, Tammy found herself on the other side. She'd done it at last!

Tammy quickly called the firefighters, but they couldn't get there for fifteen minutes.

She had to find a way to put out the fire – and fast. Tammy opened a window and floated out of the school in search of help.

She was hovering over a nearby construction site, when she saw just what she needed.

Getting through the study wall had given Tammy new confidence. Now she was ready to try her scaring skills.

The driver leapt out of his cab in terror.

Now came Tammy's biggest test. She concentrated on the truck. It was a lot heavier than a toad.

Using all her energy, Tammy lifted the truck into the air. Moments later, it was hovering above the blaze.

Tammy made one last effort and flipped the truck over. Its load of sand swamped the flames. Within seconds, the fire was out.

Whew!

At that moment, the firefighters arrived. Miss Creepy and the rest of the school weren't far behind.

The students found Tammy
lying in an exhausted heap.
"What happened?" cried
Miss Creepy.

As the firefighters made sure
everything was okay, a tired
Tammy told her story.

That evening, Tammy was
the star of a special ceremony
in front of the whole of Creepy
College. But she was too
sleepy to enjoy it.

Perhaps when she woke up,
someone would tell her she
was now a Grade A spook.

# Chapter 3

# The tale of the haunted TV

One Saturday afternoon, Glen
Goggle was watching TV.
Suddenly the set made a
funny fizzing noise and the
screen went black.

Glen's dad called out Mr. Sparks, the repairman.

You've worn it out, lad.

It wasn't my fault.

Mr. Sparks put the television in his van and returned with a battered-looking replacement.

Glen had never seen such an ancient TV set.

"It's better than nothing," said Mr. Goggle.

Glen's parents had no problems watching the TV. But the first time that Glen tuned in, something strange happened.

Hey! This isn't *Cartoon Club.*

A man in strange clothes appeared on the screen and burst into song.

Harry was a terrible singer. But he was so funny, Glen didn't mind missing the cartoons.

The next time Glen switched on, Harry appeared again. This time he was dressed as a magician.

This show was even funnier than the last. Every trick Harry did went wrong.

The useless magician made Glen laugh so much, he had to turn off the TV to stop his sides from aching.

Next day, Harry tried to dance and kept tripping over his own feet. Although Harry was funny, Glen was starting to miss the cartoons.

Glen was about to switch channels, when Harry fell forward – and came through the TV screen. Then he grew to full size before Glen's astonished eyes.

Whoops!

Glen was amazed.

"Sorry," panted Harry. "I should have taken more dance lessons when I was alive."

Glen gulped. "You mean, you're a g...g..."

"I always wanted to be on television," said Harry. "So when I became a ghost, I decided to haunt this set."

"I can't rest easy in the spirit world until I'm a star," he sighed.

Glen felt sorry for Harry. He offered to let him stay if he stopped haunting the TV.

Harry spent the next few days moping in Glen's room.

Then one afternoon, Glen showed him a ticket. "Look where we're going," he said, with a grin.

Come and watch

TALENT TIME

The Top TV Talent Contest

being recorded

Saturday October 4 / 3.30pm

at XYZ TV Studios

BIG CASH PRIZE FOR THE TOP ACT!

Harry was full of excitement. He'd never seen a TV show being made before.

Glen wasn't sure if spooks were allowed in TV studios. Harry shrank himself down so Glen could smuggle him inside.

Glen was relieved when he reached his seat in the audience. Harry peeked out as the lights dimmed and the show began.

There were singers, dancers
and comedians. Glen thought
they were great, but Harry
did nothing but grumble.

Glen didn't notice the ghost
float away. So he got a shock
when a full-size Harry
suddenly appeared on stage.

Harry pushed the other
contestants aside and went
into his act.

He sang
terrible songs...

he messed up
his magic
tricks...

and he finished
with his clumsy
dance routine.

The audience roared with laughter. Harry won first prize as the star of the show. He called Glen on stage to say thank you.

With a big grin on his face, Harry faded away.

Glen grinned too. Harry had given him the prize money to buy a brand new TV.

Series editor:
Lesley Sims

First published in 2004 by Usborne Publishing Ltd., Usborne House,
83-85 Saffron Hill, London EC1N 8RT, England. www.usborne.com
Copyright © 2004 Usborne Publishing Ltd.